Self Publish 2021

NOTHING !!!
You can do this

By GW Tolley

GW Tolley - International Author, Writer / Executive Producer of "i am JOSIAH" Movie, TV Host / Executive Producer of "What's Your Story," Self-Publishing Coach, Hearing Impaired and Deaf Awareness Advocate, Chanan Ministries (Timed In Foster Children), WRITE It OUT Program (Firefighters, First Responders, Military, and Police Officers).

About the Author GW Tolley

How did GW become the person he is today?
Where and When - Where and when you least expect Me, I will be there.

What does hearing loss, purpose, "don't be a Jonah," and a lost sheep all have in common? Let's see. Read on.

A recent situation involving my hearing was an unnerving reminder of how precious our hearing is—and brought back a flood of emotions. I am fine, but the scars are always there. A word of advice: Wear your scars with pride. I do. We cannot have a testimony without a test.

I had ear issues from birth, and that went on until my second year of high school. I was constantly at the doctor, and the medicine he prescribed tasted nasty. When the medicine ran out, the issues would come right back—and sometimes worse than before. When I was younger, they removed my tonsils to see if this would correct the issue, but it did not. **Not only did I have a hard time hearing, but my last name starts with a T, so usually, my seat was in the back of the room at school. Unable to hear, I would get bored and doodle, and my mind would wander everywhere. My significant accomplishment was Receiving a C- or even a D+.** My mom would work with me with flash cards. She would say, "You are smart and can do anything you put your mind to." There is always a way around, over, or under every situation, and sometimes you must go through it. My momma was loving, kind, intelligent, and business savvy, but that's another story if you messed with her family or children.

One day, my mom noticed I had the TV turned up loud. It was at the highest volume and could not go any higher. She returned me to the doctor and told him, "Send him to a specialist. He cannot hear." While at the ear, nose, and throat specialist, I found out I had **95% hearing loss in one of my ears**. The doctor did surgery right then and there because of the extreme situation. The doctor inserted a tube to correct the issue. They brought in a machine that was like a giant vacuum cleaner. There was a big needle. The doctor said, "I am going to bust your eardrum, and you will hear a strange

3

noise. We will vacuum out the liquid." The liquid was almost black. The noise was thunderous and nearly unbearable. They could not numb my ear, and I just had to be a big boy and tough it out. My mom said, "Be strong. I am right here with you." I did well, and she wiped the only tear from my eye.

All of this taught me to keep moving forward and be an overcomer. "Reach for the stars, but remember to keep your feet on the ground." So, with all that being said, if anyone had told me I would write a book, much less books with an s, I would have laughed at them and said, "No, not me! You are mistaken. You have the wrong guy." English, spelling, grammar, punctuation—that is not me. "Thank You, God, and thank You for my editor," I tell it like it is, and sometimes it's just the raw truth. Occasionally, that is hard for people to handle, but it is what it is.

When you have a story, and it feels like you will explode if you don't tell it, whether you like it or not, you have to get it out of your system. Release it and get it out. That is what happened to me. The stories had to come out—the pain, the hurt, the shame, the tears of sorrow, and joy. Write even when it is uncomfortable because getting it out is one of the best ways to heal. People are going to talk about you no matter what you do. You cannot control what they say or what happens, but you can control how you respond or don't respond. When you do that, you control yourself, which is powerful. NEVER let people, where you came from, or your circumstances dictate who you are and where you are going! You have a purpose; I have a purpose; we all have a Kingdom purpose.

Jeremiah 29:11, "For I know the plans I have for you declares the Lord. Plans to prosper, not harm you, and to give you hope and a future."

As a child, I was dragged to church Sunday morning, afternoon, and Wednesday every time the doors opened. I vowed when I was older that I would never go to church again. I did not go for 20 years. I was the very angry, drunk, and mean Prodigal Son. You would have never heard me speak of God. I believed He was there but I would not discuss Him. We all have a choice.

The storm of my life had begun, and I did not know until it was too late. The unstoppable chain of events started with identity theft in June 2009. Then, that led to my home being foreclosed on Christmas Eve and later padlocked. God said, "My house, built on the sand."

Excessively partying with fair-weather friends, I went down many wrong roads. My house of sand collapsed, and 98% of my possessions were donated to a charity. I was homeless and then laid off. Out of desperation, I placed an ad on Craigslist for a place to live. I ended up living with a family of nine.

Some nights, I had no food. I would microwave water to fill my stomach so that it had something warm in it so I could sleep. I ate oatmeal for two years, and finally, I dropped my pride and went to a food bank. What is ironic is that I volunteer at a food bank. I was too prideful and ashamed, and they quickly said, "Raise Your Head!" They shared they started as a client and are now volunteers. There is no shame here!

The most overwhelming challenge was losing my mom. She died four times, and on two occasions, she was gone for over 30 minutes but came back to life! There is power in prayer, and miracles happen every day.

A significant turning point was when I fell asleep while driving, and my car was headed toward a transformer pole. And a man called and woke me up and he said, "God had told me that you were in danger and to call you. Your divine life purpose is much needed in the world. I have to stay on the phone with you until you're parked." I know God saved my life.

I had to change my "Whys" into "I Trust You." I had to stop whining and being a Jeremiah. I had to stop saying, "Please take away these burdens." Instead, I had to pray for faith, broader shoulders, strength, and seeing others as God's children and not judging. I also had to learn to forgive. Giving situations to God, I started watching my words. A few words of kindness can change a person's day or life. This process was about learning to be Christ-like, selfless, unshakeable faith, hope, and love. Start listening to God and being obedient.

God has given me the strength and the courage to take one step at a time. Through this 10-year process, He made a unique way in His time. My trials have become my testimonies, and I am giving God all the praise and glory. My life has been restored and blessed, and God made His Masterpiece out of my mess.

God has revealed my Kingdom PURPOSE, and I would have never in a million years guessed it or even thought about sharing or speaking about His FORGIVENESS and GRACE.

But here I am; I have stopped fighting my calling. Don't be a Jonah (Jonah 1-4); don't be a GW; run for 20-plus years and take a 10-year learning process. Just don't is all I can say; it is painful; embrace God's LOVE and His MERCY. I share my stories through my trials, tribulations, and testimonies. I want people to see Him, not me, and God be ALL the Praise and Glory.

People have said, "We see that GW found Jesus."However, the truth is Jesus found me! Every day, I thank Him for pursuing me. I was that one lost sheep. Lost and Found!

Jesus told them this parable: "Suppose one of you has a hundred sheep and loses one of them. Doesn't he leave the ninety-nine in the open country and go after the lost sheep until he finds it? And when he finds it, he joyfully puts it on his shoulders and goes home. Then he calls his friends and neighbors together and says, 'Rejoice with me; I have found my lost sheep. I tell you that in the same way there will be more rejoicing in heaven over one sinner who repents than over ninety-nine righteous persons who do not need to repent. Luke 15: 1-7

Purpose through the pain and new eyes to see, a ministry and program created.

Chanan Ministries: (meaning Grace) Working with people without housing, less fortunate, widows, and "Age-Out" Foster Children; another word is "Timed-Out." A majority amount of aged-out children end up homeless, on drugs, abused, and a staggering number commit suicide. The statistics are overwhelming and alarming. With love and respect, we will not call the children "Timed-Out" but "Timed-IN." O goal is to assist, educate, and mentor. In return, they can educate and mentor other "Timed-IN children." Putting a stop to the cycle!

WRITE It OUT: The "WRITE It OUT" program created is for Firefighters, First Responders, Military, and Police Officers (also offered to civilians). Due to the ever of our world and increasing stress, the goal is to write painful events to get them ou' of the mind and onto paper. Then, the stories can be shredded, burned, or published Sometimes, people need someone to listen. Listen! To look into their eyes and see that they are a person.

Statistics: Suicide Key Facts from the World Health Organization. More than 700,0 people die from suicide every year. The fourth leading cause of death in 15-29-yea olds—this alarming figure of more than 700,000 children, men, and women per ye The Suicide and Crisis Lifeline is 988 and available 24 hours a day. Please make tl call.

9

Chapter 1 - Overview

Are YOU Ready to Get STARTED?

Know "YOUR WHY"
Examples of Why
What is Your Why
Putting Your Why into Action
How Will You Put Your "WHY" into Action
Know YOUR WHY
Here is the MOST IMPORTANT Part: Know "YOUR WHY"!!
When you know "YOUR WHY," it will give you direction and purpose, and it will also motivate you. Your why is the most crucial part. #KnowYourWHY

Examples of "WHY" - GW Tolley's - "WHY"
I want people to share their testimonies/stories with the Whole Wide World. WHY? Because you never know who Your Story will help, inspire, or change their life. Maybe show them they are not alone in a situation where someone else has gone through the same thing or something similar. You might give them a ray of hope. It might stop them from ending their life. We never know. It could also help you, as the writer, to release their pain or hurt. I share my story of being hearing impaired, barely passing through school, the feeling of no purpose, shame, not wanting to live, trials, tribulations, joy, happiness, and overcoming to inspire others. I am not a victim; I am a Victor. I do not want to use the word "Disability" because, in one form or another, we all have ABILITY. Sometimes, we might have to find a different way around whatever that is. Keep moving forward, no matter what challenges we face or have been through. Just keep moving one step at a time, even if it is a baby step. Without Trials, we cannot have a Testimony. If I can do this, you can do this. I am not saying it will be easy, but do not quit or give up on your dreams. Step by step and day by day, keep moving forward. See you at the Finish Line, Published Author.
Know "YOUR WHY"
Examples of Your Why
What is Your Why
Putting Your Why into Action
How Will You Put Your "WHY" into Action

What is Your Why?

Putting Your "WHY" into Action

Missions, Causes, and Charities. Have a purpose and build and uplift people. I work with many charities; it is all about giving back and building each other up. Each one of us can change the world and make a difference. All we need to do is love people with genuine compassion. One person at a time.

1 Peter 4:10-11 Each of you should use whatever gift you have received to serve others, as faithful stewards of God's grace in its various forms. If anyone speaks, they should do so as one who speaks the very words of God. If anyone serves, they should do so with the strength God provides, so that in all things God may be praised through Jesus Christ. To him be the glory and the power forever and ever. Amen.

How Will You Put Your "WHY" into Action

I would like to say one thing

If you only knew how often people have laughed or said you don't even have money to eat, how would you publish a book? I have heard so many NO's. I have listened to NO, we do not do it that way, that is not our standard publishing/printing process, that will not sell, people will not like that, people will not purchase that, we don't do that style anymore, and on and on and on I would like to say one thing: GW Tolley International Published Author. I am not arrogantly saying this. I am saying watch who you listen to.

No, to me, they are not the right people or company. Keep searching for the correct open door or window. Just because it is available does not mean it is the right one. How do you know? Ask questions and lots of them. If you do not understand, ask them to CLARIFY. If they get defensive or try to pressure, that is a RED Flag. Use Caution.

If I had taken their advice and listened to them, you would not be reading this book.

How will YOUR Story Help Others, Impact Others, Bring Change or Awareness?

Chapter 2 - Overview

GET STARTED
Topic / Story Line
Birds Eye View

You have a book idea and now what?

Where to get started: Develop a Topic / Story Line
(TIP - Use Index Cards to write your titles on and start writing)

If you are starting, here is a great way: take index cards and write your story titles (one per card) on the cards. Once you have your story titles, put them in an order that flows. You can add, remove, or place them at any given time.
In the beginning, I had writers flood, and all the stories would come rushing forward like fighting for me to tell that story first. The index cards helped with the process organizing my thoughts.

Another Tip: If you have posted stories on social media or a blog, you can see the details and the date, giving you a timeline

What is your Topic or Story Line?

____

____

____

____

____

____

____

____

Please keep it simple and specific. Get to the point of your story, and do not take people on a scenic, wordy world tour if you do not have to. How many times have you read something several times and tried to figure out the story's point? Do it if you can write your story in 56 pages versus 500. Remember the 56-page reference; I will explain it later. I will get right to the point; this is information I found out the hard way and used to self-publish my second printed book, A Modern Day Job, and the many books that followed. I hope this information I have learned the hard way saves you time, money, and mistakes and helps you become a published author.

BIRDS-EYE VIEW

Hopefully, this book will give you a birds-eye view of what is involved. You must pick a style and method you are comfortable with that works for you. Just because it suits someone else does not mean it is right for you. There is no guarantee that these tips and information will make you money. If you follow your passion, the money will not matter. Remember to enjoy your JOURNEY along the way.

Chapter 3 - Overview

Book Size and Margins
Page Numbering
Images
56 pages
Author Name

Printed Book Size and Margins

Size of your book and Margins: It is best to set the foundation initially. Book size and margins are the **MOST IMPORTANT STRUCTURE** of your book.

Why do you know your book size in the beginning? You must correct thi now because a regular-size document is 8.5" x 11" unless your book is 8.5" x 11". If you wait until the end of this process and set up the size, everything will shift, and I mean everything. Table of Content, Index, Images, Sentences, and it takes a lot of time and money if you are using some to assist you.

If book size information does not motivate you, maybe the following statement will get your attention: **Due to the size of the book, it will no be available in the following countries.**

You have eliminated book sales in other countries, equating to lost money in your pocket. Do I have your attention now?

I did that with the "Sacha Healings and Miracles" book. Size 8.5"x6" It is not only printed in English but also Spanish. That is two books and more than one country. Remember the tip: Keep it Simple and Simplest. Fancy and Cool could cost you money.

(TIP - Layout Tab: Page Set-up and Margins)

> **Click Page Set Up Tab**
> *Paper set up*
> *Manage Custom Sizes*
> *Book Size (Example 6" x 9" or 7" x 10")*

Now you have the size set up, let's set up the margins. **The margins are significant.** Think about this: the book's left side is where the pages' binding happens, and there needs to be a bit of additional space. Here is how I set up my margins.

Click Layout Tab
    Click on Margins
    Custom Margins
    Top   *.5*
    Bottom   *.5*
    Left   *.75 (Binding Side)*
    Right   *.5*
    Gutter   *0*

MAKE SURE TO GO BACK INTO THE SETTING TO SEE IF THIS PROCESS IS SET UP AND SAVED.
If you are using Mac Pages
Document Tab
Select your Page Size
Choose your Page Orientation
Header and Footer uncheck unless you are using this format

    Top   .5
    Bottom   .5
    Left   .75 (Binding Side)
    Right   .5

Setting up your document size (Book Size)
Document Tab
Printer & Paper Size
Example (7.00 x 10.00 inches)

If you do not see the size of your book, like this book is a 7.00 x 10.00, and that was not an option, try this.

File (Tab)
Page Setup
Paper Size

Page Numbering: While setting up the size and margins, this is also an excellent time to ensure your **Page Numbering is ON**.

Images: If you can use your Images/Photography or Royalty-Free Images, do it. Make sure to read the fine print wherever you get the images. I like to use my images/photography or create my images, keeping things more straightforward and fewer people in the mix.

56 Pages: Remember above. I said to remember this reference in getting to the POINT - Don't Ramble or take people on a wordy scenic tour. Here is why the 56-page reference, when using Amazon/Kindle to publish your book "Publish Size Book," is 56 pages, depending on the size. I hope this takes a little of the pressure off of you.

Author Name

Are you using your real given name or a pen name?
What is your Author's Name?

My Author Name Is: ________________________
Your author's name has a good ring to it.

Write the vision and make it plain

I am a published author

Date: __________

POP QUIZ:

1. What is the Size of You Book going to be? _____________

2. Why is setting up your Book Size and Margins Important?

____

____

____

3.) What are the Margins Settings for the following:
Top _______
Bottom _______
Left _______
Right _______

4. How many pages do you have to have to publish a book using Amazon / Kindle? ______

5. Fill in the blank: Remember to enjoy your ______________ along the way.

Chapter 4 - Overview

Book Covers

There are so many options to book covers. Be Creative
You can Paint Your Book Cover.
You can have a Digital Image (Picture or Graphic Design)
You can use a Drawing for Your Book Cover
Mixed Media: Sand, Glitter, Beads, Cloth, Picture or a mixture.

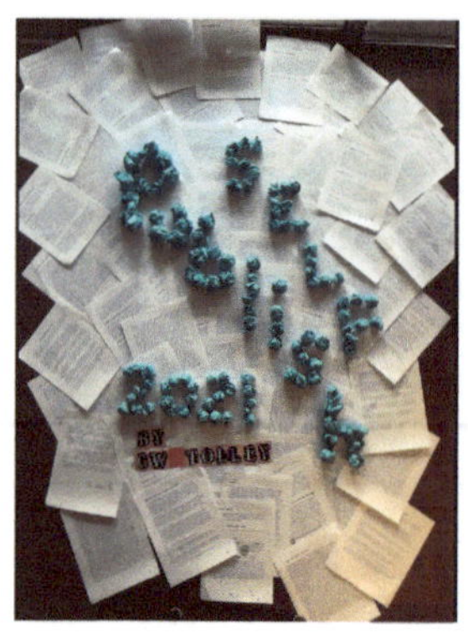 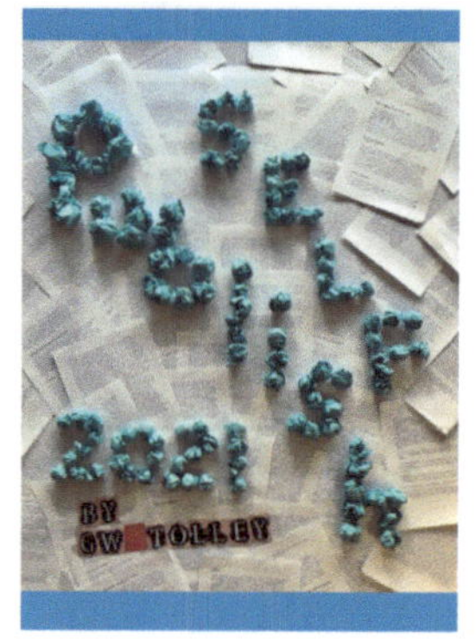 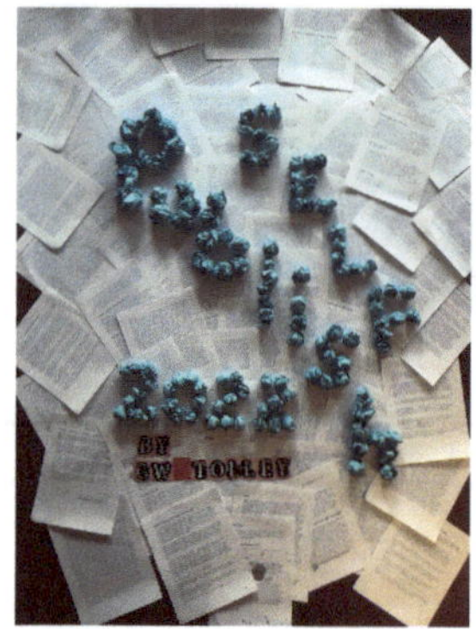 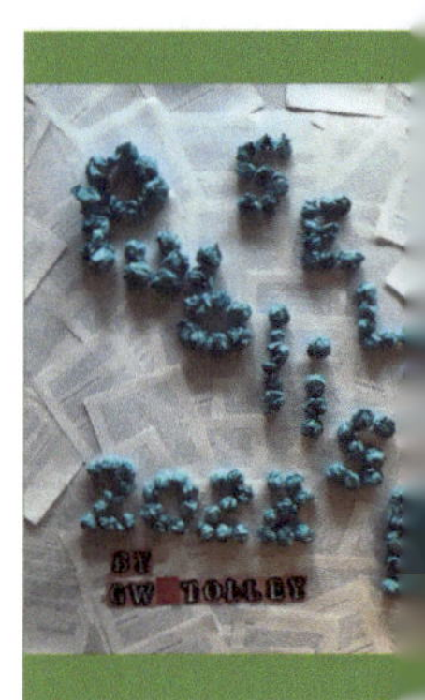

How about using edited pages and Paper-wads?

Actual Fact: SELF PUBLISH 2021 Book Cover was made from 300 Edited Pages from A Modern Day Job. Spread all over the floor in a section about 8 feet by 6 feet. The next set was two different sizes of Blu paper wads to spell the title. A Stencil that I used to paint my name on two prior books. During that process, I had to turn off the ceiling fan and the AC unit, which was hot during the Florida summer. Once completed I stood on a tall dining room chair, stretched out as far as possible towar the center of the masterpiece, tried to keep it level, and took the picture with my iPhone 7 Plus. I took several pictures in case something was of Here is the kicker: I was led to change the number 1 made with paper wads at the end of 2021 and make a 2 out of paper wads for 2022. All of this took place at the beginning of 2021. I was not sure WHY then. There would be much more crucial, helpful information for me to learn during the next 12 months and share with you. Technology changes so fast, and knowledge is power.

Be Different ~ It's Your Book ~ Be YOU
Well, as different as you are allowed to in the publishing world. Sometimes, there are restrictions and rules.

A Modern Day Job book
The Image on the Front is also the Back Cover for several of my book covers. Why, you might think or ask? You can see the book title no matter what side the book is on. Talk about great marketing and advertising. That was not my idea; that was all God's.

Example of Painted

(TIP - If you need or want a high-resolution file, a Reprographics Company can Scan your image; the estimated cost is around 45 dollars)

Example of Digital Images

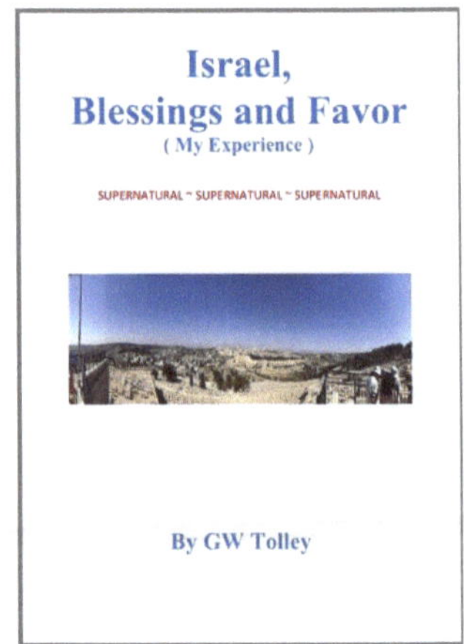

Example of Graphic Design - English / Spanish

Graphic Design Book Cover

I wanted to use the image I created on my phone with the book title and author name, and it took some time and a lot of effort to make this work and change it to a high-resolution image. When working with a graphic designer and getting the best work possible, know what you want and have all your information ready. **Remember, time is money, changes can be costly, and you get what you pay for.** You can use the images for marketing, posters, artwork, bookmarks, and branding. Just because you use a FREE Vector File and Images does not always mean you own the rights, and it could lead to a lawsuit and royalty fees.

NOTE: Some Book Cover Apps do not always convert into suitable printable files for some printing companies.

Example of Graphic Design using
Amazon/Kindle and **Book Cover Creator**

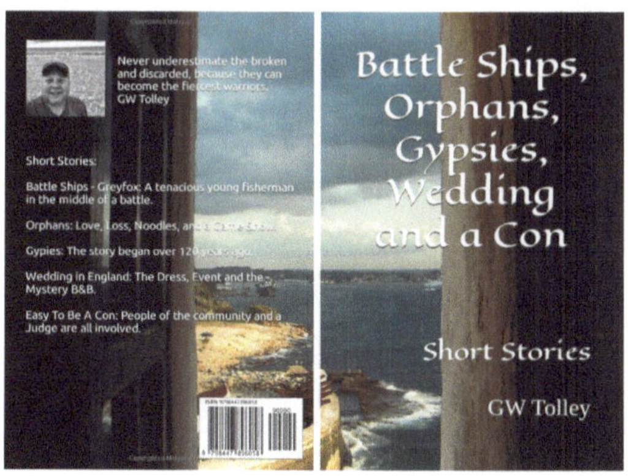

FUN CREATIVE QUESTION TIME

1. What Media Are You Using for Your Book Cover
      Paint
      Graphic Design
      Digital Image - Picture
      Drawing
      Mixed Media: Sand, Glitter, Beads, Cloth
      Mixture

2. What are Your Colors going to be to Match Your Story?

____

3. What is Your Style or Design to go along with Your Story

____

____

____

4. Will you use the Front Cover Image as the Back Cover Image? Or a front cover with vocabulary and a picture of you as the back cover

____

____

____

5. Are you getting excited about being a Published Author?
YES - NO - MAYBE - NOT SURE - Talk about it below

____

____

Chapter 5 - Overview

Types of Self Publishing and Tools

In this book, I will give three publishing examples:
Publishing Company
Using a Printing Company
Amazon/Kindle

Self-Publishing Company

I used a Self-Publishing Company for my first book, Comforting Messages From Heaven. They are Christian publishers and needed to see what I would print before publishing my book. I had to send them images and the file, and they approved it. Once the material and images were approved, the next step was picking a printing package. What services did I need, like editing, graphic design, press releases, marketing, book cover design, etc? Once through that process was the payment, the money. My first book cost 1,800 dollars, and I made payments for one year. I did a GoFundMe Fundraiser and raised 350.00 dollars. Sometimes it works, and sometimes it does not. Do not get mad if people do not buy into your dream. It is not their dream; it is yours. Be thankful for what help you receive. I was assigned an author website portal, and I could upload the manuscript file, images, and book cover. The book would not be published until I paid the final payment. The 1,800.00 dollars was for the ISBN (International Standard Book Number). ISBN is a numeric commercial book identifier, a unique number for every book. That price included a barcode and putting the book on Amazon. This pricing does NOT include the editing, graphics, press release, marketing, advertising or book cover design; these are additional charges.

The PROFIT was random depending on WHERE the book sold (book store/company and country) and the SALE PRICE they set. The profit range of .35 cents, the lowest and the highest, was $3.50. Usually, there is a minimum payout amount ($50.00-$75.00) before they cut you a check or direct deposit. Also, remember this is income, and you will pay taxes. Make sure you read the fine print. Ensure the images and content you use in your book are 100% your property. Look for that information before you sign or agree to anything.

Cost: Yes, there is an investment

Printing Company

The easiest way to explain this process is to send a completed edited book file with your ISBN (International Standard Book Number). ISBN is a numeric commercial book identifier, a unique number for every book. Copyright information and Barcode. (Estimate $25.00 Barcode, $184.96 ISBN, and $45 to $65 to register your Copyright) I will go into further detail, but please hold these costs in your thoughts for now. You will need to send your book cover image (is your cover going to be gloss or matte), book size, what type of book cover, paperback or hardcover, paper thickness and or quality, color or black and white, type of binding (saddle stitch, perfect bound, plastic comb binding, staple), and how many copies you want or their minimum. There is also the factor of digital or offset printing.

What capabilities or limitations does your printer have, like if they do the binding in-house or outsourced? Also, if they are a small, medium, or large printing company, this plays into their purchasing power via discounts, buying groups, and rebates. One way or another, all of these things are factored into the total final cost (Your cost per book). Again, this is the book cost only. As I said, depending on your printer, many things affect the printing price. The bottom line cost can affect your sales price and profit margin. Quantity: the more books you want printed, the lower the cost. As I mentioned above, the other things that will affect the book price are size, hardcover versus paperback, number of pages, images, paper thickness, font color, and when you want or need your book. All play into the cost. It is best to find this out first and have a guide of all the factors that go into the cost. Get several quotes and see what works best for you. You can also search online. See who you like working with the best. All of this is very important.

Remember, I talked about Book Size and Margins a lot, and there are reasons. Well, book two, A Modern Day Job, is where I learned a lot of valuable hard lessons. I sent what I thought was the "Final" Finished File to the printer and was in for a big eye-opening surprise. The finished Book Size was to be 7" x 10", but the file size I sent was 8.5" x 11". Do you see the big major issue? Everything shifted, and this was not a fun time. Time is money when you are paying editors. The next mistake was the Binder Margins. Wrong margins caused a complete book shift. My printer needed a Binder Margin of .75 on the spine side. The book had so many "FINAL" and "FINALS" of the book that it was not funny. We started putting the time beside the date to keep track of which 'Final' draft we were working on.

I will also tell you to beware of some Apps that provide Book Covers because some printers can not convert the files.

When you are looking for a printing company, look for a professional company with excellent customer service and personal interaction to assist with your printing needs. Read the company REVIEWS, shop around, and get quotes. Remember, you are not just printing a book but building a business.

What other printing capabilities are available: book markers, business cards, catalogs, calendars, greeting cards, invitations, business cards, tee shirts, merchandise, direct mail, and fulfillment services. Things to ask about or look for is a state-of-the-art printing facility that specializes in digital and offset printing and printing experience/expertise.

All of this information is a lot to take in. Still, it significantly benefits you, resulting in high-quality products and the security of knowing they will handle any project to your complete satisfaction.

COST - Depending on all the information above and the quantity. There is a medium to more significant investment.

Amazon / Kindle

Amazon / Kindle direct publishing kdp.amazon.com is another way to publish your book via e-book, paperback, or hardcover. They provide you with an FREE ISB Number (International Standard Book Number), Book Cover Maker, Print on Demand, and Ship to your customers.

Here are a few examples of things you are in control of:
Category or Categories your book placement
Set when you want to launch your book
Sale price
Marketing - optional - additional cost

You can order one copy or 999 copies through your author center.

Here is an OVERVIEW of KDP.Amazon.com

Book Content: You upload your book content, and I usually upload it as PDF. There are FREE creation tools for children's books, comics, manga and educational content.

Book Cover: There is a book cover creator, or you can use your own book-designed creative book cover image.

The next step is to add your description, keywords, and categories. These three are very important! Description tells the reader your potenti customer /client what your book is about. Keywords help people find your book in their search or via the category.

Free ISBN (International Standard Book Number) is a numeric commercial book identifier. ISBN is a unique number for every book. I will go into a little more detail as you read further on.

Now that you know the OVERVIEW, here is the drilling down into the process. Here are the things you need to think about and to have ready. I will use the Printed Paperback Book Details as an Example.

Language
Book Title and Subtitle Optional
Series - if any
Edition Number - if any
Author Name
Contributors - if any
Description
Publishing Rights - You own the copyright and publishing rights or Public domain work
Keywords - 7 Keywords
Categories - 2
Adult Content - No or Yes

Content Section:
Use your own ISBN or Amazon FREE ISBN
Publication Date - Optional

Print Options: Black and white with cream paper
Black and white interior with white paper
Standard color interior with white paper
Premium color interior with white paper

Trip Size: Book Size **(Stay AWAY From Non-Standard Sizes)**

Bleed Setting: No Bleed or Bleed (PDF Only)

Paperback cover finish: Matte or Glossy

Upload Manuscript

Upload Book Cover or Create Book Cover (Launch Previewer)

The summary will also show your printing cost.

Paperback Rights & Pricing

Territories: All Territories (worldwide rights) or Individual Territories

Primary Marketplace amazon.com or other
Pricing, Royalty, and Distribution
Terms & Conditions

Save as a Draft or Publish Your Book
COST - ZERO
BUT I WOULD SUGGEST GETTING A COPYRIGHT

Note To Self
If writing a book is on your heart, mind, and soul, then do it no matter what anyone else says or does. There are Dream Killers everywhere. Sometimes, they say things like, "It will not sell!" or "You cannot do that!" The best thing is to keep it quiet and tell no one. Once it is published, you can talk and promote all you want. It is your dream, and that is all that matters. Tell yourself not to take it personally! I followed my dream and published some books while others played games or watched TV. The difference between a writer and an author is that an author is published.

ISBN and Barcode
The self-publishing site I used was Bowker Identifier Services MyIdentifiers.com . The cost was $25.00 for the Barcode, $184.96 for the ISBN, and registering your copyright. There will be an additional cost for Rights Licensing. Again, this does not include editing, graphics, press releases, or book covers.

To complete this process, you will need your book size, weight, and sell price.

Copyright

Register your work and make sure you copyright it. The process is not complicated as it sounds but very important. Go to CopyRight.gov. How to Type the Copyright Symbol on a PC Keyboard: Hold the ALT key down and type 0169 on a regular laptop. If you use a Mac, you must hold the 'Option' key and press 'G.'

Title

Let's start at a place that will save you time and effort. The Title or Theme carries through your book, and the **next two steps are critical**. Very SIMPLE but very important.

Web Search

Search your title and see if it is connected to something X-rated or might have a wrong meaning. You never know, and it is better to be safe than sorry.

Domain

You have web-searched your title and are on to the next step. If you are in the thinking/planning stage, just starting your book, in progress, or completing your book, you are now ready to purchase your title domain. I use www.GoDaddy.com to buy my domains. Type in your title and see the results. DOUBLE CHECK YOUR SPELLING and recheck it. Trust me, I know from experience. You will find the following outcomes: Available, Available spelled the wrong way, Not Available, or the Title Is In Use, and the seller that owns the domain wants thousands of dollars. If it is available and spelled correctly, purchase it now and do not wait. Here today, gone tomorrow! I would suggest you add the Auto Renewal option. You can always change this at any time. You will receive renewal reminders if you choose not to add this feature. I like auto-renew, and it gives the option to cancel. That is just me; do what is best for you and your budget. If you change the title later, the most you have spent is $2.99 to $12.99.

If your writing is in the planning or starting stage, you can think of a new title. If your work is complete, what do you do? Adding a LETTER to your title might save the day. One letter might save you work hours, screaming, frustration, and tears. Example: My second book is called A Modern Day Job. That title was not my first title choice. The first title I chose was "Modern Day Job," and I found out the domain was unavailable. My title fix was easy by adding an 'A' to the title, but this is not always true. You might have to change the words around and have the same meaning. You will have to see what works best for you. If not, you might have to think of a different title. Before you think of this labor of love as a NIGHTMARE, breathe and do nothing. You might think you want to redo the almost-finished work or just be ready to give up at this point. Stop, breathe, rest, and think. A new day or a few days and new eyes may also help the process. Whatever you do, do not give up. Birth this baby.

Purchasing your title domain from the start could save many issues, which is why I recommend doing that.

These are just my thoughts and suggestions. I would recommend purchasing the domain for your author's name. Now you have your book title domain and your author name domain. You are on your way. If you do not purchase the domain or domains, you might be singing this tune: www.SomeonePurchasedMyAuthorName.com

I have heard horrifying stories of projects finished and the title domain belonging to someone else or a company. That company is an enormous corporation, and there would have been a lawsuit. A graphic artist designed that book project, and that redesign cost additional money and time. Please save time, money, and effort and purchase your book title and author domain first.

I did not stand on the sideline and not give a warning. I strongly recommended that the domain be purchased several times. Ignoring this advice, or not prioritizing it, is a costly mistake. However, I did not say, "I told you so". The hours, money, blood, sweat, and tears that can go into a project can be overwhelming.

One of my biggest irritations is when someone sees something and says nothing. Sometimes, they do after something happens and say, "Yeah, I saw that." That type of person is not a true friend and someone I don't want around—just my opinion. Surround yourself with quality people who want the best and uplift you.

Folder, Save, and Backup

Folder, save, and backup sounds simple, but setting up a folder and saving your work is necessary. I would suggest emailing the document to yourself and keeping it on a zip drive or Google Drive. You never know what can happen. TRUST ME… strange things have happened: a virus, hard drive issue, power outage, deletion of the wrong file, or a misplaced file, and everything lost. I would suggest a Battery Back Up / Surge Protector to be on the safe side.

Speak Your Book

Some programs allow you to speak into a microphone, and it will write your story onto the screen. You will have to double-check and make sure your words translate correctly. Descript and Grammarly are good programs. Technology constantly changes; join a writer's group, share, and listen.

Spelling, Grammar, and Punctuation

Scrivener, Celtx, Grammarly, and Word Edit programs are great ways to check spelling, grammar, and punctuation. No matter how often a document is checked and double-checked, something is overlooked or missed. We are all human, and we make mistakes. It is not the end of the world; correct the issue or issues and re-upload the document if you publish it on Amazon (Paperback or E-book). Warning: watch out for autocorrect.

Language Options

I published two books in English and Spanish (Sacha Healing and Miracles) and (Five Short Stories: Battle Ships, Orphans, Gypsies Wedding and a Con). I know enough Spanish to be dangerous.
A couple of children's hospitals and several charities I donate books to are so happy to receive books in Spanish. They said they did not have any Spanish books for the children. That was a big surprise to me. Have you thought about doing your book in another language?
What language would you choose?

Chapter 6 - Overview

FONT and Color
Solution Provider
Speaking about others
Slang Words - BIG Words - DECODE
Target Audience
Book Category

It's all about the FONT

It's all about the FONT
Not everyone has 20/10 or 20/20 vision. I use font size 14 and Times New Roman in the body. 18 bold underlined Times New Roman font on the story titles. CAN YOU SEE ME NOW? I like to see things clearly and not have to squint. I do not use any light colors or a faint thin-line font. I do not use any fancy designer font either. If people try to figure out the words, they might stop reading. The goal is to have peopl read and enjoy your work of art. Some schools do not teach cursive writing, and som people can not read cursive writing. I do not use cursive or a squiggly font or loop to loop, which can throw people off. Fancy-swirling fonts might be hard for them to read. I want people to see what I have written clearly; it takes time, money, and effo People tell me that reading with their glasses for a while gives them a headache. The said they enjoyed reading the sizeable bold font that they could see clearly and read without their glasses.

Solution Provider, Problem Solver, Feelings

Is your book providing a solution, or are you a problem solver? Solve a problem and become a resource. Inspire and be uplifting; the change starts with us. If you bring up a PROBLEM, then provide a SOLUTION

When speaking about others

Use caution when writing about others, and BEWARE about mentionin people because people can quickly figure out whom you are speaking o Use caution about using their real names unless they permit you. Think about how they would feel if they read what you wrote about them if it was terrible. Put yourself in their shoes; what would you think? Probab be mad. Do not talk about other people's sins or mistakes. Please keep i clean. Be humble and kind. If that is not enough, they could bring a lawsuit against you.

Slang and BIG Words

Know your audience. If your book is intended and targeted for all ages and everyone, you might want to avoid abbreviations, acronyms (LOL), slang, and big words your reader will have to stop and look up. They will lose their focus and the point you are trying to make. If your reader can not DECODE or has to use a dictionary to translate your work, what's the point? Not only that, but you could lose a client to purchase your next book.

Target Audience and Marketing Direction

Everyone does not like the same things and is not from the same background or culture, and people have different tastes and likes.

Example:

Faith, Encouragement, Faith-Based, Presenting the Gospel, Religious and Spiritual.

Fiction or Non-Fiction

Male

Female

Children

Youth

Middle Age

Older

Example: It could be a movie for 9-12-year-old girls

Now break it down:

Male Under 25 / Male over 25

Female Under 25 / Female over 25

When you have all the target audience details, you will also have your marketing info / direct and how to package your project.

Book Category

The category is critical. Make sure you place your book in the correct categories. When you are looking for something specific, you do not want to do an endless search and dig for what you are looking for; be specific and laser-focused. Make it easy for your audience/buyers to find you. Find the common denominator for your target market. Being too broad and using the shotgun approach will not assist you here. Focusing on your target audience also helps your rankings and sales. If you are writing a cookbook, your target audience is not everyone, as we would think. If you believe everyone will purchase your book, some people do not like to cook, bake, or like every subject. So make sure you list your book in the right target category and not a general category. A broad category could have millions and millions of books on that topic. One of my books is in a category where there are 7 million other authors and over 6 million in the category. It sounds simple, but stay focused and laser-targeted on your category. Find your NICHE.

I am thankful you found my book or books. I appreciate your support, Thank you.

Chapter 7 - Overview

Co-authors and Special Guest Writers
Foreword
Will you do me a favor?
Reviews

Co-Authors and Special Guest

When someone is a part of the story or stories in the book, they share with their friends and family, expanding the number of people who read your book / their story. It adds an element of creditability to the story. Th other side of the story or adding to the story can be an essential ingredie and a special sauce. Please ensure they know what topic you are writing on and what you want and need from them, as well as guidelines and, most of all, when required. Let them know of your Hard Deadline, and i you want to remind them, do that; let them know upfront if they do not have the story or the chapter, you will not wait on them. Ask them not tc share the storyline and No Spoiler Alerts. If you treat this as a hobby, then that is all it is. Business is Business. As the saying goes, The Show Must Go On. If a person adds their view to a story or even a co-author c co-authors, they only share or confirm the information; most of the time they will be paid or not paid. Let them know this upfront. If you wish tc pay them, consider paying them a flat fee, and they have no rights to your book or book sales. It is best to have a legal document so everyone understands and there are no hurt feelings or misunderstandings. Amazon / Kindle pays the primary author directly, and you will pay the taxes on the earnings. The last thing you want is to cause tax confusion, so think about this when you ask people to co-author. Ask a lawyer and an accountant. Also, only one person is the primary author. Amazon allows one author and one co-author.

I have heard stories of people asked to assist with books, and they have not worked out the details, and the person asked to help did not ask any questions. The excitement of working on a project becomes a chore, more hours than they want to put into the project. One person has the website, one has the images, and one has the writing, and something goes wrong, or they are not going in the same direction. Two years or longer, and the project is still not finished; it is a complete nightmare. Little pay, no pay, no name recognition, and people's feelings hurt and could damage friendships or lawsuits. Please do yourself a favor; don't go down this road; it is nasty and bumpy.

Foreword

Ask an established published author or a professional to write your foreword; this adds creditability to your work. If they say no or do not have time, please respect that. Say thank you and find someone else, or move on without a foreword. Find someone who adds value, likes, and agrees with your subject. If they say yes, remember they are now a part of your body of work. People have their options and robust options that you might not like. Take this into account before just asking anyone. Be open-minded and listen without being offended. Think about their suggestions, and they could give you valuable feedback. After all, you did ask them for assistance and their valuable time. Make sure they know the timeline of when you need this completed. They are reading your book. As in the above paragraph, ask them not to share the storyline and No Spoiler Alerts.

Side Note: Make sure you spell the foreword correctly, not forward.

Will You Do Me A Favor?

Ask 5 to 10 people to read your book. Tell them you are not asking them to rewrite your book. You are looking for feedback. Do they have storyline questions, or do they not understand something, like holes in the story or character development needing something additional? LISTEN to the feedback. Do not argue and get all mad. LISTEN! If something confuses them, it more than likely confuses other readers. You now have the chance to add or correct the issue. I know it is your baby, but don't take it personally. Fix the issues and move forward.

Save yourself time and a headache; do not ask people who can not give direct answers. Stay far away from the: Well, I don't know, I am not sure, the Yes people, it's excellent, someone that deflects questions or provides vague answers.

If they say yes, make sure to give them a deadline, or they might not read it, and by giving them a deadline, they could say I don't have time. That is okay; we all have busy lives. It is not for everyone, and we can not get mad at people or our families because they do not see the vision or dream. Ask someone that has time, and you value their option.

Reviews

Also, ask if they will write a review for you. It could only be two lines: short, sweet, and right to the point. The last thing you want to do is rewrite someone's review, and they say, "I did not write that, or that is not what I said." Not everyone likes to write, or they might not think they have perfect spelling, grammar, and punctuation.

If they do not want to write or they don't like writing, try this: ask them questions. Write down what they say.

What did they think of the book?

What did they like?

What did they not like?

How did the story or stories make them feel?

Why is the book different from others they have read? Or why not?

Did a story help them or something they can relate to?

Was the outcome what they expected or unexpected?

Did they find purpose or meaning? If yes, have them explain.

Would you recommend the book to friends and family? If Yes, ask why and see what they tell you. If not, why not? Do this in a pleasant tone. Do not be upset; listen and take notes. This information is your time to understand and make changes. It could be just that person's taste. Be open-minded and listen and write.

Ask the questions and then send them the information to see if you can use it. It is their words and their review. DO NOT mislead them by giving fluffy, flowery answers because the honest reviews will tear you apart, and they will not think twice. It is their hard-earned money you are messing with. They will not get their time back.

You want to have positive, truthful feedback. How often have you heard a movie or a book review and thought it is the best thing since sliced bread, and it is the worst? You can not make everyone happy; some people are never satisfied, but you want honest feedback. People see right through fake reviews.

Deadlines also hold you accountable for your launch publish deadline. Make a Plan and Stick to it. Make a flow chart, write it on your planner, calendar, or grease board, and do whatever it takes and what works for you. It would help if you had the reviews before your launch date.

Chapter 8 - Overview

Additional Cost
Packaging / Shipping
Self Fulfillment
Business Cards and Point of Contact
Taxes
Website

Additional Cost

Packaging type (box, bubble envelope), tape, printing a packing slip, shipping label, postage, and packaging cost comes out of your profit. Gas to pick up unless you have it delivered; remember to factor in the delivery charge, if any. If the shipping company is not picking up packages, write down mileage to and from and keep gas receipts. Time, we often forget our time.

If you hire freelance help, it will also factor in. Ask your accountant for help with these additional items.

Packaging and Shipping

The oversized cardboard box or package adds to your client's shipping cost and could cost you the sale. Having the right size packaging and not having shipping damage are the keys. I did a web search and found a Kraft Bubble Mailer that is the perfect size is lightweight, and has added protection. I also found several packaging companies that can do cardboard shipping packages. If the packaging is too large, the cost is more expensive; don't go cheap = damages.

Self-Fulfillment

Why would I want complete control of packaging my products? I have control of what I place in the box with my book. If I want to promote another product or book, I can do that. I am fully in control of my company. I have other friends who are authors, and we can cross-promot our products. You decide who you want to work with and what products you want to promote.

Business Cards and Point of Contact information

My business card is my book's front and back cover with the details and purchase information in the middle. Remember to use a font size that people can see without a magnifying glass and no fancy fonts.

P.O. Box address
Web Site information
Email that reflects my domain and author name.
Phone Number: Smart Line Phone Number for business, not my persona
phone number. I know when that line rings, it is business. The cost is
around $9.99 - $12.99 a month, and I can set the hours and the message

Taxes

Company versus individual/hobby. When you have your books printed, you will pay tax on the books unless you have set up a company. Contact your CPA/accountant and see what is best for you before you run to the city and county office to set up a business.

Website

When you are in control of your website, you are in control of your clients. You have the email addresses, phone numbers, and addresses. You can send out upcoming products and events if they opt into emails. When you create and release a blog, they are the first to know and feel like part of the family. You will create belonging if this is done by sharing and not hard-selling fashion.

Chapter 9 - Overview

Write and Rewrite
EDIT - EDIT - EDIT
Final – Final – Final – Final
Launch

Write and Rewrite

 I Write and Write and do not stop to go back and Rewrite during this writing process. If I think of something, I make a note and will return once I finish writing. Now, if I am in the same sentence or paragraph, I will go back and change or rewrite. But I have found out the hard way that adding something here or there changes the flow or can even confuse the reader/editor. We have to put ourselves in the reader's shoes. Just because we understand does not mean they will know or understand our point of view. Even when I stop in the middle of a project or take a weekend or a few days off, I have to get back into the process or the train of thought. Maybe this process does not happen to you, and you can jump from page to page, topic to topic, and do what is best for you and your writing process. We are not all alike.

EDIT – EDIT – EDIT

Self-edit as much as you can. I will read it several times before handing it to an editor. There are programs, but they do not catch everything. Who is editing your book? Will you hire someone to edit? Ask an English teacher, There is Fiver, or do a web search for editors for hire; ask people if they know of an editor, but make sure they do not edit you out of your book (been there, done that).

Have someone you trust who does not know the stories you are writing about and see if they understand what you are trying to get across to your reader. I have friends who love to read, and they read fast, and I let them read my books. Sometimes, they will see mistakes. I will read the book aloud with my editor, and we will see if something is unclear or needs to be re-worded, if there is a mistake, or if the flow needs to be changed. You want things to flow effortlessly and clearly. We could check and double-check and triple-check, and someone will find a word, autocorrect, or something. It is what it is, and you can not overly stress about it.

Final – Final – Final – Final ??

Make it easy on yourself. Trust me! There has to be a point where you have to let it go and set it free.

Launch

Launch date: You do not want to launch your book when all the TOP New York Best Sellers and the other 10 million people launch their books. They have way too much marketing money and big publishing companies in place to even try to compete with them.

Launch time: You are in control of the time, and if you launch and post at 3 am, who will see it? Maybe 11:30 am when people are going to eat lunch? Also, consider your time zone; that will make a difference. Mak your marketing dollars count for you, every penny.

Pre-launch: Remember to post the date and time of your book launch ALL your social media. Send emails, call, and text.

MAKE IT A LAUNCH EVENT: Have a launch party? **Post Pictures** Tag People, Tag Places and Things. Maybe a Launch Lunch? Sunday

Launch Brunch? Speaking of pictures, before the camera snaps a picture, I ask that they do not make any hand gestures, rabbit ears, no peace signs, etc. What is okay today could be wrong tomorrow. No funny faces unless it is a funny face picture. Hand gestures are in here because while a picture was just about to be snapped, someone made a hand gesture, and it was not a bad sign, but the person said you can't make that sign now; it means something else.

THINK OUTSIDE THE BOX: If you have your book printed locally, when you have copies, search for a bookstore or a place where your book would complement their products and maybe have a signing launch party. The event would draw attention to their store or business and could be a win/win for sales. Make sure to have all the details worked out prior. What do they want for selling your book? What is their cut? In some stores or businesses, you can only leave on consignment; they are not responsible for lost, stolen, damaged, or missing merchandise. Maybe place a few books and check on them often. In one location where I had placed books, they hired a new management, and I went to check on them, and the books were gone. No one knew what happened to them. Loss of merchandise is something to consider. That will be a loss write-off; check with your accountant. You will learn as you go; not all situations are the same. Do what is best for you and what you feel comfortable with. Think outside the box: Farmers Markets, E-bay, Book Fairs, Meetup Groups, Book Clubs, and Charity events, and give a nice donation or a percentage from the sales. Remember, it is for charity; don't be greedy. You are using this as your marketing and helping a good cause simultaneously. If shops or people say NO, say thank you and keep moving. It was not a good fit. Remember to be Kind, Happy, and Joyful. You will find the right fit. You never know who knows who, and you might just run into these people again when you least expect it.

Share: Ask people to share. They will not share unless you ask. Do not get upset or be mad at them if they do not share.

PRE_LAUNCH testimonials: These are so important. Post the testimonials of the people you had read your book, written a story, or co-authored. You can also use the reviews/testimonials in the book. But remember, the people paying to read your book will tell the truth in their reviews.

Example of a Book Launch
A Modern Day Job was an international launch unveiled in Israel on
August 19th, 2019, in the City of David.

Chapter 10 - Overview

Set up Social Media
Swag Bags and Events
Business Card Tip
One Thing could lead to another
TV, Radio, Podcast, News Papers
Interviews (Golden Rule)
Brand
Affiliates
For Sale
Corporate Seal
Images
Find the Time and Notes
Distractions
Reminder Sign

Social Media

THINK OUTSIDE THE BOOK. Now that you have your title, I sugges
creating a page on all social media. Again, you can permanently delete
the page. Remember to add a word or letter tip if the page is unavailabl
Do not forget to create a YouTube channel. People love short videos
(REELS) and try to keep them under 1 minute. Fast, sweet, and right to

the point. Keep the excitement up, and remember to breathe and smile. Remember your hashtags (#) and appropriate tags about your subject. Every post, blog, podcast, and video should ALWAYS LEAD PEOPLE TO YOUR WEB PAGE OR WHERE YOUR BOOK IS FOR SALE. ALWAYS

Swag Bags - Events

Events that you can add your advertising media, sometimes there is a cost. Look for events to attend or have a table that matches your audience. Examples include media summits and film festivals. Speaking of events, here is a funny story, but it was not amusing then. I was at the International Christian Film and Music Festival in May 2019, a massive event with around 10 thousand people attending, and I was displaying my books. I had my media information in the swag bags, 10 thousand (my story via a flyer, book-marker, postcard, and business card), so I had 40 thousand items. I had left the booth for a few minutes, and while I was away, a man left their business card on my table when I returned. And it was from a TV Executive, and on the back of the card was written: "Come see me." I asked the information booth the location of their booth, and "They said down the hall on the right." I go down the hall, look for the Name and Logo, find the table, and ask for the man. He said what do you want with him? I said he left a card on my table, and I showed him the card. He said, "Why does he want to speak with you?" I said, "I do not know; that is why I am here." He said what do you do? I thought he was being the guard, and I did not understand. I shared my story with him, which was the more extended version. He said, "I understand why he would want to speak with you." I said, "Do you know when he will be back?" He said, "I do not know; you are at the wrong booth." I was in shock, and now all the questions made sense. There was only one slight difference in the company's name; the colors and logo were very similar. He said, it happens constantly, and I would like to speak with you about my TV Station". I said sure, may I have your business card. God has a sense of humor. It's not the first time I have ended up in the wrong place, but it is always the right place. When this happens, I have learned not to let it rattle me or leave me embarrassed; it is a divine appointment. I am there; be present, be calm, explain what I am doing and who it is for, and let God be God, and He will do the rest. It has worked out every time, and the people ALWAYS remember me. Stand Out – In A Good Way at an Event.

God opened a door for me to attend a Texas Film Festival and Media Summit in February 2021, and I walked through that open door. He (God) wrote a book in two days (Monday and Tuesday). The title is "i am JOSIAH". He did something different this time. He had me use the index Cards, but He drew pictures with the titles on the back of the index cards (Story Board). The book was then edited, graphic designed, three tee shirts designed and printed, 100 book-markers designed and printed with my email address and personal cell phone number, and 20 books printed. I picked everything up on Friday. All of this happened in 4 DAYS. ONLY GOD CAN DO THAT. Talk about standing out, what a way to market, and a conversation starter. On the 4th day, it was Red Carpet Day (Dress Up Day). I did not have an "i am JOSIAH" tee shirt, but guess what??? Everyone said Hello, JOSIAH. How are you doing, JOSIAH? That is some fantastic God Marketing! BOOM! Way to go, God!

Even people I did not personally meet knew the branding "i am JOSIAH" just from seeing me. I meet so many people, and as I was meeting additional people, I would say, do you have an "i am JOSIAH" book-marker? If they said no, I knew to share the story and give them a book marker. When God said to provide them with a book, I did. God's fantastic marketing led to being invited to speak on TV Shows. One posted on my Social Media Feed about meeting me with their side of the story (Testimonial), a picture of "i am JOSIAH" book and the book-marker with a personal public invitation to be on their TV program. Glory be to God.

Media Summit book launch example: "i am JOSIAH" was **revealed** at Content2020 Film Festival and Media Summit at Capernaum Studios in Poolville, Texas, February 1st - 4th, 2021

Book to Big Screen

Speaking of "i am JOSIAH" book, it was written in storyboard form and will be on the big screen. Where the Book Ends, the Movie Begins. Bringing a true story to life! See you at the movies. Books are door openers sometimes, and we never know where they will lead us.

www.iamJOSIAHMovie.com   Check it out, and please Subscribe.

Business Card Tip

You can meet hundreds of people at these significant events, and trying to remember everyone can be a blur. Another tip God taught me was when you meet someone, you receive their business card, and you want to connect with them later, fold their card in half; this leaves a crease, and even folded flat, you will see the crease and remember to reach out to that person. If the person mentioned something in conversation or you need to connect to that person, add additional fold long ways on their card.

IMPORTANT Contacts: If the person does not have a business card and some prominent executives will not carry cards, you can open your Contacts on your phone and ASK to add them. I will add the event where I meet them. Once you finish, take a screenshot so I have them in two places. Sometimes, I ask to take their picture to add to the profile. I know this sounds bold, but no one has told me no. But I do not do that in a pushy way, and you know if you are pushing or intruding on their comfort zone. I never want to do that. I like to ask questions, and most people like to share what they do. If they are not in the mood to share or are a secret agent, you can also share with them what you are doing or your project and ask them if that is something they do or who the contact person is. If they say no, it is not; ask them if they know of someone or a company that would be a better fit. If you do not wear out your welcome and are kind, they will remember you and your story. You never know who that person will tell your story and share your contact information with.

One Thing Could Lead To Another

One Thing Could Lead To Another

Being an Author and books can lead to speaking engagements (main speaker or guest speaker), radio or podcast guest interviews, TV guests, or a TV host. You could start a podcast with the Spotify app (formally Anchor Podcast) or one of the other podcast apps. There are Film Festivals worldwide, so pitch your story to an entertainment company (Film or TV) to be made into a movie or television company for a TV show. Write a script for a play or a Broadway show. You never know if you don't put yourself out there. All they can say is yes. Follow your passion and your "WHY" you never know what will happen.

I will tell you that Movie Makers / Movie Finance wants to see the existing intellectual property with multiple income streams. They want to see a book or book (page count around 90 to 110 pages), merchandise, podcast, something with a track record, following, and most of all, sales.

The question is: what do you want to do, and where do you want to go?

TV, Radio, Podcast, News Papers

TV, Radio Stations, podcasts, and newspapers have requested copies of my book, books, or a list of my works. The reason for the request is so they clearly understand who I am and what I stand for before they go any further.

Brand

I traveled internationally and saw a fast-food Golden Arch without word on the sign. I knew what it was. Build your brand!!

Affiliate and Streams of Income

Affiliate allows you to promote other people's products or services and earn a commission from each sale. Affiliate programs typically have ver low overhead, meaning that you can quickly start making money and start earning passive income and additional income streams with minim effort. Add Affiliates and products to your book.

Affiliate Example:

PureTrim natural health products are the safest, most effective, and best on the market today. The products are based on the time-tested herbal wisdom.

Corporate Seal

Give your book a custom look and feel with a Notary Embosser Seal. Make your client feel special because you took the time to specialize and put your seal of approval on your labor of love. Directly embossing to the book page or use the silver or gold foil. The silver and gold foil is an additional cost, and adds a classy touch.

Images

Turn your book cover or images into sellable artwork, cards, calendars, tee shirts, etc. You never know what will take off.

Find the Time

Everyone's life is busy. During books one and two, I worked full-time and traveled the entire state of Florida and southern Georgia. My days start early and end very late, arriving home late Thursday night and leaving on Tuesday. While at home, there are house chores. I understand being busy. When on the road and an idea would come to me, I would write on notepads, scrap pieces of paper, napkins, the back of business cards, or whatever is handy. While at home, there is a notepad beside my bed, in the living room, beside the shower, or in the kitchen. You never know when a thought will come to you. I would take all the information and put it into a folder. The ideas would begin to bubble, and the key is to take the time and let them unfold onto paper or in a document.

Distractions

As you start to write, there will be distractions. The doorbell or phone will ring, people you have not heard from in years, text, emails, children, and pets, you name it, and the distractions will come at you from all directions. As I wrote one of the books, Hurricane Dorian, catastrophic

Category 5, one of the strongest on modern record, was predicted to hit Florida. Keep writing and moving forward one page at a time.

Reminder Sign

There is a sign on the wall over my desk.

One Page At A Time
~ Write ~ Publish ~ Inspire ~

What does your Reminder Sign say?

Chapter 11 - Overview
Audio Booth 101
Audio Booth Example 101
acx.com requirements

AUDIO BOOTH 101

Life is never dull, and there is always something to learn. We can learn the hard way or the easy way. I prefer the easy way, but that is not always the case. Here, enter Books on Audio. I checked the recording studios around town, and the prices ranged from $75.00 to $100.00 per hour to do the audio recordings. I was planning on doing three books, which is a lot of money. I get it: equipment, knowledgeable staff, building overhead insurance, etc. I could have hired a narrator; that would have cost more money. The public library has a studio, and you can sign up for classes and then use the equipment, but it has not reopened since the COVID-1 pandemic. So what did I do? I researched, asked everyone I knew, watched YouTube videos, and prayed.

ONE LAST CHANCE
By GW Tolley
LISTENING ON
audible

i am JOSIAH
by GW Tolley
LISTENING ON
audible

AUDIO
SELF HELP 2021
BY GW TOLLEY
LISTENING ON
audible

Building an AUDIO BOOTH 101

I went to the home improvement store and purchased 2x2 boards.
Eight cut to 5 foot lengths (Top and Bottom Frame)
Four cut to 7 foot 6 inches (4 Corner Posts)
Eight Simpson Strong-Tie Heavy Duty Strap 6" L x 1-3/8" W 12 Ga
Wood screws and bungee cords and Zip-Ties
Every blanket and bedspread I could find.

I was building this by myself, and the bungee cord was my helping hand, holding things in place until I could permanently get them into position. I also Zip-Tied the post to the desk for extra support. The floor lamp was involved in an accident during the first raising-the-roof attempt and received significant damage, but it still works.

Here are a few other items you will need to take this mission
Quiet space away from windows and door
Floor Lamp to see in the dark box
Desk Lamp to know what you are reading
Fan when not recording for airflow because the Air Conditing unit is off
Computer with Garage Band / Audacity
Comfortable non-squeaking chair
Comfortable clothing
NO Jewelry or Watch
Water - Nothing that will dehydrate you
Battery Back-up
Good Earphones to hear the playback
Microphone with a Pop Filter or Foam Windscreen

Files will have to PASS ACX.Com Requirements

Why the following information matters.
I had my share of FAIL, a Large Thick Folder of FAIL.
Let me tell you a lawn mower, leaf blower, delivery truck, trash truck, mail truck, cars, emergency vehicle, fan, Air-Conditing, squeaking chai dishwasher in the next room, clothes, breaths, a cord moving, jewelry i picked up by the microphone. You will be amazed at what the microphone will pick up.

I used both GarageBand and Audacity to correct recording issues.

Audio Booth Example 101

It is not pretty, but it worked

Audio Book One: From what I know now, the first read of ONE LAST CHANCE took 4.5 hours for about 1 hour of audio. I was learning, stopping, starting, and all of the other learning curves, and there were plenty of them. Then I had a friend look at the file, and he moved some of the sections, and you guessed it, messed up an entire file. There was no undo or un-save. I did not tell him what he did because he was trying to help me. Crying and getting mad does not help. I had to re-record the entire book; the silver lining was "extra practice."

NOTE: Audible Audiobook Square Cover

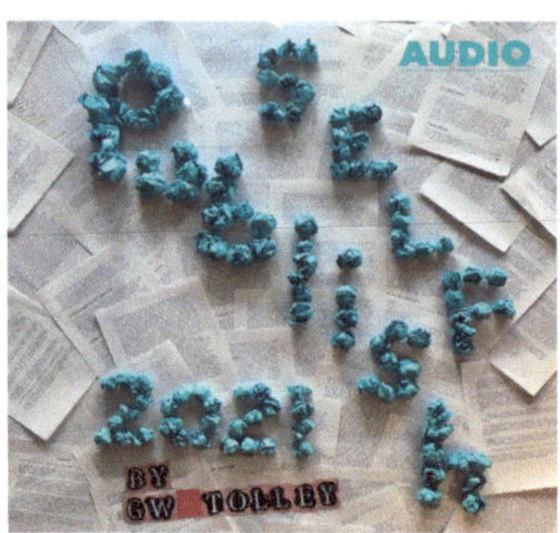

acx.com requirements

Before starting the ACX Audio/Audible process, you must have an Amazon paperback book or Kindle E-Book. Once you upload all your files and it shows passed, a screen appears Final Results in ten days. The ACX process put me to the test. This process took me six months and how many failures. I have a folder of failures; I cried, stressed, ate, and pray the entire time.

Chapter 12 - Overview
Words of Encouragement

Pep Talk: Write, write, and get your stories out of you and on the page! FINISH WHAT YOU START!

Focus: Please do not compare yourself to others; do not compare what they are doing or have done. Keep your focus on Jesus. He has put His Special DNA in you, and there is no other you.

Integrity: We all make mistakes in life; own up to them. If you lose your integrity, you have lost everything.

Keep it Real: People can see right through smoke and mirrors. Remember to Keep it Real.

Pity Parties: Stop having pity parties and joining in with others and their pity parties. I AM NOT GOOD ENOUGH, THIS IS TOO HARD! Get to work!! Say, Got to run, goodbye. Stop having the pity party prayers.

STOP with the Excuses: In the world that we live in today with spell check, grammar, and formatting; you have no excuses.

What is STOPPING YOU? Nothing but YOU! Get out of your way—type, type, and type. Philippians 4:13 I can do all things through Christ who strengthens me.

Do what is best for you: You have three choices: self-publishing company, printing company, or Amazon/Kindle. Do what works best for you. You can be an Author/ Business owner.

There is a fourth choice: You can do nothing.
Nothing today is nothing tomorrow. The choice is yours, do something.

ABLE and AVAILABLE: God can and will use us for His Glory when we are ABLE and AVAILABLE. God has Opened Doors that only He can Open. When that happens, walk through it and remember to give Him ALL the praise and glory.

Stories Lost: How many lost stories because no one took the time or effort to write them down and share them with their families? Generations of stories vanished like a vapor. The next generations of children will not know their heritage/lineage and stories. Do not be the Next Stories Lost.

Author: Being an author allows you to share your stories and testimonies and maybe make a difference in someone's life for the better. The one plus or advantage it has is the ability to open doors and doors that might not have opened.

Somebody: Some have told me, "Being an author makes you somebody." The Bible tells us in Genesis 1:27 that God created man in his image; in the image of God, he created him; males and females created them. We are extraordinary.

Request for God?:
If you have a HUMBLE request for God, what would it be?
Do you believe God could do this?
Yes, God can do all things in His time, not ours. God works through people who think they are powerless, but ALL their trust is in Him. Talk to God about it. Remember not to put a cap or limit on God.

PRAISE: Start giving praise for what you have. Speak as if it is already complete in Jesus's name. Praise and give God ALL the Praise and Glory. There is no I in God. You are a child of the Highest God. Act Like It! Read Philippians 4:13

Remember: IT IS NOT ALWAYS ABOUT THE MONEY. The question is, How will you use your platform to make the world a better place?

EVERYONE HAS A STORY, and THE WORLD IS WAITING ON YOURS

Other works by GW Tolley

Comforting Messages From Heaven - Book / Journal
Description: This book is Eighty-eight inspiring pages filled with original poetry and Bible verses paired with beautiful photos. There is also a place to journal your thoughts or write notes.

Israel Blessings and Favor
The first-time international traveler sets his sights on a faraway destination: Israel. See what unfolds as GW travels alone in this foreign land. Get ready for a wild ride for what is about to unfold.

Sacha Healings and Miracles (English and Spanish)
A true story about Sacha: when Sacha was a baby, she was so small and had to have breathing treatments. Growing up, she had to have several surgeries and had a life-threatening situation. God is the greatest Healer and performing Miracle.

FOCUS on GOD's PROMISES
We must be laser-focused and right on the target; that is God.
Are you having issues with Mental Clarity and Listening?
Are you Fearful? What are God's Promises? Did you know Words are powerful? The M-Word, MONEY. Have you lost heart? Are you Confused and thinking, "WHAT IS GOING ON"? If so, it is time to Rise and Shine; it is a New Day. Walk into the Kingdom of God. God chooses us, and the Lord spoke a Blessing. It is time to keep advancing, moving forward, and focusing on GOD'S PROMISES.

ONE LAST CHANCE
A true story of an unexpected chain of events will leave you wondering what is happening and what just happened. The very wealthy and famous are not immune and cannot run from the outcome of this ending. Tears and screams turn to a quick laugh, and you will become infused with the story before you know it. And by the end of the story, there will be a decision that only you can make. ONE LAST CHANCE, and then there was none.

i am JOSIAH
The story begins with a hard-working middle-class family doing everything possible to keep food on the table and the lights and water on. In one event, a runaway car going down a steep mountain almost takes three of the family members' lives. One of the children's illnesses nearly leaves them deaf. Name-calling and bullying were too much to overcome for this child, and it almost took their will to live. Overwhelming challenges and events led to a lifetime of anger, hurt, bitterness, drinking, heartache,

and just about removed what faith there was. Nothing was left When the storm stopped, and everything hit rock bottom. When the storm cleared, God was the rock at the bottom and, this time, a new solid foundation. Only God can change a heart and restore faith, hope, love, peace, and purpose. As you read this book, it raises a question: "Are you a JOSIAH?"

A Modern Day Job

My story is on the right side of the book, and you can write on the left side with your prayers, thoughts, or story. Do not let your stories end with you; share them with your family or the world. The stories in the book are not in any particular order, just like the random events in my life. I had so many stories to tell that every time I started to write them down, they would flood forward all at once. I could never get the book started. I had a dream, and the instruction was to write the story titles on index cards and place them on my sliding glass doors. When I woke up on Sunday morning, November 18, 2018, I started writing the story titles on the index cards as instructed. typed as fast as my fingers could and did not worry about spelling, grammar, or punctuation. I wrote for 10 to 12 hours daily until Wednesday, November 21, 2018. The book was not complete just yet. The editing part was the next step. Editing was completed on August 12, 2019, and sent to the printer at 10:56 pm. The printer had the proof ready the next day for me to take to Israel and unveil on August 19 at The City of David.

GW's Final Thoughts

If God asks you to do something, DO IT! Make sure to do it just as He asks you to do it. God is all about the details. Look at how he asked Noa to build the Ark, detailed in every way. Sometimes, it does not make sense to us at the time, but it will in time (God's Time). Remember, if God said to do it, do it, and don't second guess God or get in His way. God knows best, so give Him all the praise and glory.

I have become comfortable with being UNCOMFORTABLE

GW Tolley

Let's Chat for a Minute

Let me ask you a question. A critical question: if you should die today, are you 100% certain that you are going to Heaven?

If you should die today and stand before God, and He asked you why He should let you in His Heaven, what would you say?

Did you know you can be 100% certain you will go to Heaven? You know you can understand, and here is how. In 1 John 5:13, the Bible says, "These things have I written unto you that believe on the name of the Son of God; that ye may know that ye have eternal life." Here's how you can know.

In Romans 3:10, the Bible says, "As it is written, There is none righteous, no not one," in verse 23, "For all have sinned, and come short of the glory of God." That means I'm a sinner, and that means you are a sinner, also. Most people do not realize the seriousness of sin. God is Holy, and sin separates a sinner from God.

This verse shows how serious it is! In Romans 5:12, the Bible says, "wherefore, as by one man sin entered into the world and death by sin; and so death passed upon all men, for all have sinned." The word "death" doesn't mean dying and going to the grave; it means separation from God. Until our sins are forgiven, we are separated from God on this earth and will be separated from God forever and ever in a place called Hell. This is the punishment for our sins.

But the story doesn't end here! In Romans 6:23, the Bible says, "For the wages of sin is death, but the gift of God is eternal life through Jesus Christ our Lord." The words "Eternal Life" mean more than living forever. The words "Eternal Life" in the Bible means to live forever in Heaven.

Notice being saved is a gift; it's absolutely free! You can't buy it, work for it, or be good enough. It is free! It would be as if a friend went to the store and purchased you a present. They paid for, wrapped it, put a bow on it, and brought it to you. They did everything for you; all you have to do is receive it.

That is what Jesus did! He left His home in Heaven, came to earth, died on the cross, shed His blood, and paid for your sins. He did everything for you; all you have to do is receive it. Romans 5:8 says He did this for us while we were still sinners.

Most people think they have to stop doing everything wrong before God will save them. But God loves us as sinners, and Jesus died for us. When Jesus died for you, He made it possible for you to have forgiveness of sins and eternal life with God.

But just because Jesus died for you does not automatically save you. You must ask Jesus to forgive your sins.

Now, do you admit that you are a sinner?

Do you understand that sin separates you from God?

Do you believe Jesus died on the cross for you?

Would you like to be forgiven of all your sins and know 100% you are going to Heaven? Then, this is what you need to do.

In Romans 10:9-13 the Bible says. Now, "whosoever" means you. "If you shall call upon the name of the Lord, you shall be saved."

Then, according to the Bible, if you asked Jesus into your heart right now, He would save you forever! Wouldn't you like to do this? If you trust Jesus to take you to Heaven when you die, pray this prayer.

"Dear Jesus, I know I am a sinner. I believe you died for my sins, and God raised you from the dead. Forgive me of all my sins; come into my heart today and live forever. Give me a home in Heaven when I die. Please help me to obey you. I mean this prayer with all my heart!"

Romans 10:13 says, "For whosoever shall call upon the name of the Lord shall be saved." Then, according to the Bible, you are saved, and if you were to die today, you would go to Heaven!